Dad 10.0

"ONE WORD, ONE ACTION, AND ONE DAD, CAN CHANGE A CHILD'S LIFE FOREVER. ONE CHILD CAN CHANGE THE WORLD"

15 Ways to be a More Effective Dad and Still Watch the Game

By Ott Harrison Jr.

ISBN 9780692502464

Dedication

I dedicate this book to God, and my Lord Jesus Christ. Thanks to my beautiful wife, Angela Harrison for your encouragement and inspiration. Thank you, Barbara Harrison, Ott Harrison Sr., Lauren Harrison, Gabriella Harrison, Fred Harrison, Desire Harrison, Art Harrison, Saundria Whitfield, Quevelle Gandy, Ethel Gandy, Cecelia Waters, and Anthony C. "Tony" Massengale for your awesome support.

Love,

Ott Harrison Jr.

Table of Contents

Forward

Ott Harrison Jr. has written this book for every man who has children, or expects to have children. It makes the case for why the role of fathers may be the single most important factor in the *life-success* or *life-failure* of any child. By focusing on 15 ways to be a more effective father, every dad can *step-up* and share quality time with their kids using proven ideas that will make a difference now and in their future. Dad 10.0 is the essential how-to handbook of practical positive action steps for what to do and why. It is a tough but, encouraging practical guide that can be read in one sitting, then referred to again and again to make sure every dad can provide what his child wants and needs to succeed.

This book should be required reading for every young man in high school, every expectant father accompanying his wife to the maternity room, and every dad that wants to be an effective father but, may not know where to start. It is useful whether or not dad lives with the mother of his children. If separated from their children or is separated by military service, incarceration, divorce, or for any other reason but, still wants to be a father, active in the lives of his kids.

Dad 10.0 shows the connection of fathers and daughters, not just fathers and sons. It also points out the benefits of being present physically and emotionally, being knowledgeable about how to interact with your child, and the value of being patient and keeping your sense of humor. For fathers who are married, the book shows the payoff of a father helping his wife to manage parenting, household, and financial functions.

Without going deeply into the academic research available, the book shares the consequences of dads being absent from or uninvolved with their children. National statistics trends gives us reasons why fatherless children is in greater jeopardy for mental-emotional disability, poor physical health, lack of self-confidence, educational failure, criminal activity, failure in life, and maybe worse.

I have known Ott Harrison since 1998, in the context of church ministry and family life. Long before he had children of his own, his work and volunteer experience helped him develop a father's heart. Like a compassionate drill-sergeant and a high scoring player-coach, Ott is providing a playbook to help dads help their children win in the game of life.

Dad 10.0 is a call to action for new fathers, fathers who have been out of touch with their children, overwhelmed by the circumstances of their marriage or family life, or just needed a way to get a new start on fatherhood. It is God-centered without being preachy, and doesn't back off of the spiritual insights that impact fatherhood. It is an urgent, important, and necessary message for this generation of fathers.

Anthony C. "Tony" Massengale, Sr.

Pasadena, California

How to Use this Book

This book was written especially for Dads, and for those who want to encourage men to be more effective fathers and role models. I use the analogy of a flower shop to describe how to use this book. A flower shop can be a beautiful place to visit. The main reason for visiting is to select flowers for someone special. My opinion is that everyone should in their lifetime give someone a flower or two. It is an awesome experience to see a person's face shine with joy when they receive them. When you enter the flower shop you are looking for flowers that will convey your love and gratitude. Most flowers are beautiful, but you will probably only select a few.

Select wisely from the principles and ideals in this book. As you apply the principles and ideals, watch your children's faces light up and their lives change forever.

About the Author

The author, Ott Harrison Jr., is the husband of Angela (25 years), and the Father of twin daughters Gabriella and Lauren (14). He has been instrumental in training men to be more effective fathers. Ott has worked with children, youth, Royal Rangers and men ministry for over 20 years. Ott has been a professional school bus driver for 15 years and a professional driver for 20 years. He has worked with children of all ages and abilities.

The Purpose of the Book

The purpose of this book is to equip and encourage the current generation of men/fathers to be a part of what I call generation Dad. That is a generation of fathers who are committed to stepping up their involvement in their sons and daughters lives. Dads, we can make a difference in our children's lives. This book is a tool to help us make that difference.

Definition of a Father or Dad

A Father or Dad is the male parent who takes on the awesome responsibility of taking care of a child.

Two Statements and a Poem

These are short, simple, straight forward, but powerful statements that convey the fact that Fathers are very important to our children.

A Son's Perspective

Dad, you are my hope and future. When you are not present, I feel hopeless and my future looks dim.

A Daughter's Perspective

Dad, you are my security and first love. When you are not present, I feel insecure and my first love is absent.

This is a poem about a young man whose Father was present, but later, the Father was absent.

Identity

By Ott Harrison Jr.

Dad I see you

In the mirror I see you

In the mirror I see me

I see you outside washing the car

I see you when I get in trouble

I see you when I play sports

I see you when I need correction and encouragement

I see you when I need help with homework and school projects.

I see you when we go camping

I see you when I am happy and when I am sad

In the mirror I don't see you

In the mirror I don't see me

In the mirror I don't see my identity

Chapter 1

Present

Present and Accounted for Sir!

Present: To be in a particular place, to be near or nearby, to be available, (Webster's dictionary)

For better is a neighbor that is near than a brother far off. Proverbs 27:10 KJV

"If you want something done well, do it yourself." ~ Napoleon Bonaparte.

A myriad of maladies. Fatherless children are at a dramatically greater risk of drug and alcohol abuse, mental illness, suicide, poor educational performance, teen pregnancy, and criminality. Source: U.S. Department of Health and Human Services, National Center for Health Statistics, Survey on Child Health, Washington, DC, 1993

Dad, we must be present. Dads are what I call super soldiers. We fight specific battles. Win victories for ourselves and for our sons and daughters. A Dad must be disciplined in all aspects of his life. He must focus on the prize and the wellbeing of our children. Forget the past failures and focus on your awesome future. As a Dad, we must be able to say with great confidence, "I am present and accounted for, Sir."

As a Dad, there are no reasons to be absent and uninvolved in the lives of our children. We are saying by being present, not only am I alive but, I am doing the job of a Father despite the obstacles and adversity.

Dad your presence and involvement is very important for the healthy development of your intelligent sons and daughters. Do not, I repeat, do not believe anything to the contrary. Your children need you. It is no longer acceptable for a Dad to come home every day from work and just relax. That is, to sit down on the cough, watch a game, drink a beer, eat dinner and go to bed. You have two jobs now.

Your second place of employment is your home. As a super soldier you must break through, bursting down any walls that tries to hinder you from participating. Either you just do it, or you ask God to help you and then do it.

If you have young children, you must help your wife or the mother of your children take care of your sons and daughters. You may need to feed babies, change diapers, bathe, cook, and, even clean the house. If you have older children, assist them with homework and school projects. At the end of the night, volunteer to get the children ready for bed, tell bedtime stories, and say a little prayer.

Communication with children is very important. By communicating with your children you are able to set boundaries. Provide structure and a safe environment for your children to grow, mature, and flourish.

Dad, when you are present you are teaching your children by example several important things:

- A good Dad takes responsibility in the care of children.
- How a Dad is supposed to act.
- Dad is a person, but, he is not perfect.

Dad, your presence and involvement is very important for the healthy and whole development of your intelligent sons and daughters. Do not, I repeat, do not believe anything to the contrary.

Call to action:

- Be involved, get in their faces figuratively and literally.
- Be willing and ready to work with children.
- Change diapers, cook, and clean if needed.
- Communicate with children. You talk, they listen, they talk, and you listen.
- Pray with children, tell bedtime stories that teach morals, responsibility and create laughter.
- Read to your children.

A simple bedtime prayer.

Father God, in the name of Jesus, thank you for (the child or children name). We ask you to give (the child or children name) a good night sleep. We thank you that the angels watch over (the child's or children's name). In Jesus name, Amen.

Chapter 2

INVEST

What is Your ROI* ?

*Return on Investment

Invest: To involve or engage especially emotionally (Webster's dictionary)

Be not deceived; God is not mocked: for whatsoever a man soweth, that shall he also reap. Galatians 6:7 KJV.

"A Mind is a Terrible Thing to Waste." ~ The United Negro College Fund.

School Behavior: Adolescents in intact families are less likely to exhibit problematic behavior in school, and tend to have higher levels of academic achievement.

Compared to children living in intact families, peers living in (1) single mother families, (2) single-mother families with cohabiting partners, and (3) married families with stepfathers were more likely to have ever been suspended or expelled from school; more likely to have engaged in delinquent activities in the past twelve months; more likely to have problems getting along with their teachers, doing homework, and paying attention in school; and more likely to have lower grade point averages. On the Peabody Vocabulary Test (PPVT), an indicator of <u>cognitive development</u>, children living in married-parent families with stepfathers and those living with married biological parents performed similarly; however, compared to adolescents in married biological-parent families, those living in single mother families or those living with <u>single mothers</u> and their cohabiting partners tended to fare worse on the PPVT.

Wendy Manning and Kathleen Lamb, "Adolescent Well-Being in Cohabitating, Married, and Single-Parent Families," Journal of Marriage and Family, Vol. 65 (November 2003), pp. 876–893.

Your child brain is a super magnet for massive amounts of information. The truth is that all our sons and daughters are extraordinary beings, created by an awesome and great God. When He created them, He had a check list one hundred miles long. He checked everything off and He did not withhold any of his creative ability when creating them. They were one of His best designs. Our children use their eyes, ears, nose, mouth, and brain to experience the world by receiving massive amounts of information. Their brain takes this information, organize, analyze, and use it for present and future use. This information is used to develop them and their lives.

Children see everything. The most import thing that you must know Dads, is that you are very important to your children healthy development. They need your interaction, input, and support. They need your humor, instruction, structure, discipline, encouragement, and love. Don't be the missing link in their development. Be there to deposit and invest seeds of greatness, love, hope, and possibilities. You don't have to be perfect, just honest, and real. You are their dad for life.

In 2002 my wife and I had beautiful twin daughters, Gabriella and Lauren. I had the great opportunity to be at home for the first two weeks of their precious lives. After two months of working alongside my beautiful wife Angela, I realized, I was looking a little rough. I needed a haircut and a shave. That day I went to the barbershop, then returned home. As I entered the house, I greeted the girls who were sitting in their rockers. They immediately started crying. They did not recognize the new me.

Immediately, I let them know that they do not have to cry, "it is Daddy." I came to the conclusion that information they had collected in the last two months was not matching what they were currently experiencing from me being present and accounted for.

I was already important to their developmental and learning processes. Dads you are important to them even at that early age of two weeks. They had been receiving pictures of what dad looked like and what he does. Dad you are important, take your responsibility seriously. Invest aggressively and reap the dividends of your labor.

Call to action:

- Take your role as father seriously and with joy.
- Take time to be a positive influence at the early stage of your children's development.
- Read to them, hold them, help take care of them.
- Spend as much time with them as possible.
- Don't be the missing link in their development. Be an effective Dad today.
- Remember, being a dad is a great responsibility and honor.

Chapter 3

FORGIVE

The Power to Forgive is the Power to Live

Forgive: To stop feeling anger toward (someone who has done something wrong): to stop blaming (someone) (Webster's dictionary.)

Then Peter came to Jesus and asked, "Lord, how many times shall I forgive my brother or sister who sins against me? Up to seven times?" Jesus answered, "I tell you, not seven times, but seventy-seven times. Mathew 18:21-23 KJV

"When angry count to ten before you speak. If very angry, count to one hundred." ~ Thomas Jefferson.

They have a saying in the real estate industry, which says, the most important thing about a piece of property is, "location, location, location". One of the most important aspects of any relationship is the principle of forgiveness; you must forgive, forgive, and forgive. Any relationship not incorporating this concept is doomed from the beginning. It is absolutely important Dad, that you forgive and teach your children to do the same. There are two people you need to forgive, yourself and others. Teach your children to forgive, themselves, others and you. Yes, dad we are not perfect, we make mistakes and need to be forgiven. Let your children know that God expects us to forgive others and He freely forgives us.

Forgiveness is important for a healthy and whole life. Studies have shown that unforgiveness can be a contributing factor in physical and mental illness. Holding onto hurts is like having a case of food poising, in order to live healthy your body must get rid of it ASAP.

A good way to start the process of forgiveness, is by saying out loud, "I forgive (name of person) for (what the person did or did not do)." Forgiveness is your responsibility; no one can do it for you. If you come to the conclusion that you have hurt someone, you need to take responsibility and ask that person to forgive you. This can be a humbling experience, especially if they reject you or your offer. If someone has offended you, take the initiative to talk to that person and try to reconcile the relationship or remedy the situation.

Dads, teach your child to forgive, by example and by instruction. Let your child know that if a person keeps hurting them, keep their distance from that person, and consult their parents or an adult for intervention and further instructions. It is important to forgive. The bible clearly states that if you don't forgive others, God will not forgive us. Matthew 6:15.

Call to action: Forgive, Forgive, and Forgive.

Chapter 4

Effective

But Not Destructive

Effective: Producing a result that is wanted: having an intended effect (Webster's dictionary)

"To thine own self be true, and it must follow, as the night the day, thou canst not then be false to any man." ~ William Shakespeare.

Be not deceived; God is not mocked: for whatsoever a man soweth, that shall he also reap. Galatians 6:7

"The cynic says, 'One man can't do anything.' I say, 'Only one man can do anything. 'One man interacting creatively with others can move the world." ~ John W. Gardner.

Dad you are number one. When you hear these words it sounds very selfish, but what I am saying, it is important that you, take care of yourself, so that you can be effective in taking care of others. If you are seriously ill, you become less effective as a father. You have no effect at all if you are six feet under. (Dead)

If your physical, mental, spiritual and financial condition are excellent, you can better assist your sons and daughters in winning in their lives. There are three keys to being physically fit:

- Have a regular exercise regimen.
- Eat healthy.
- Drink plenty of water.

It is also important to get annual physical exams. If you notice any mental or physical issues address them as soon as possible.

Three keys to being spiritually fit:

- Have a church home.

- Have a daily devotion, reading and prayer time.
- Have a relationship with God and His son Jesus.

It is important to take care of any mental issues that may arise as soon as possible. Mental issues can wipe a Dad out and make him ineffective. If you have signs of depression and or abnormal anxieties, please see a doctor. I know of fathers who have lost their families due to mental issues and harmful addictive behaviors.

Last but not least, a dad needs to be fiscally fit. He must have a source or sources of income, for example, job or own a business. He must invest in himself and be more marketable, by increasing his education and or skills. This enables you to increase your income and take care of the needs of your family.

Dad it is important to be mentally, physically, spiritually, and fiscally fit. We need to be in shape to care for our children, in the most effective way.

Call to action:

- Start drinking plenty of water.
- Eat healthier.
- Exercise.
- Get annual physicals.
- Include your sons and daughters in your healthy activities.
- Invest in yourself to increase your ability to handle your financial responsibility.

Chapter 5

<u>Volunteer</u>

<u>Another Way to Be Present</u>

Volunteer: A person who does work without getting paid to do it, a person who voluntarily undertakes or expresses a willingness to undertake a service (Webster's dictionary)

Married persons volunteered at a higher rate (31.9 percent) in 2012 than did those who had never married (20.7 percent) and those with other marital statuses (21.3 percent). The volunteer rate of parents with children under age 18 (33.5 percent) remained higher than the rate for persons without children (23.8 percent). Bureau of labor and statics 2012.

"People may doubt what you say, but they will believe what you do." ~ Lewis Cass.

Volunteering is another way to be present. It has been said that it is not about the quantity of time, but the quality of time you spend with your children, that is important. This is partly true in the sense that it is better to spend one hour riding bikes and talking, than watching television for ten hours and not talking. More quality time together, is better than less quality time together. This is a true statement. Children need to spend time with you doing things that create positive memories and great learning experiences.

Children equate the time you spend with them, as a reference of whether or not you care about them. You must spend time with your children. It is important to them, and it should be important to you. If it is not important to you, change your mind today. This shift in your thinking will change your life and the lives of your children forever.

One interesting way to spend time with your children is to volunteer at events that your child participates in, for example, school, after school programs, children's ministry, sports, girl scouts, boy scouts, etc.

Volunteering is a wonderful way to spend time with your children. It allows them to see you in a different light. It lets them know that you care about what they are involved in, it also allows you to see what your child is exposed to on a daily basis. There is a possibility that you might not like what you see, which allows you to implement some changes that will help your child grow. Dad, show up at the following events to let your children know you care about them:

- Father's Day events at school.
- Open house at school.
- Parent teacher conferences.
- Attend their sports events and performances as much as possible.

Remember Dad, you are important to the healthy development of your sons and daughters. Quality time, volunteering, and attendance at a Child event creates a wonderful atmosphere for the growth of your child and their relationship with you.

Call to action:

- Spend time with your children, be creative in the activities you choose.
- Read to your children, have them read to you.
- Help with homework whenever possible.
- Take walks or ride bikes with your children to school whenever possible.
- Spend individual time with each child.

Chapter 6

TEACH

Dad on Demand

Teach: To cause or help (someone) to learn about a subject by giving lessons, to give lessons about (a particular subject) to a person or group, showing how it is done, to cause to know the disagreeable consequences of some action, to impart the knowledge of, to instruct by precept, example, or experience, (Webster's dictionary)

Fathers, don't exasperate your children by coming down hard on them. Take them by the hand and lead them in the way of the Master. Ephesians 6:4 MSG

"It is one of the beautiful compensations of life, that no man can sincerely help another without helping himself." ~ Ralph Waldo Emerson

A noted sociologist, Dr. David Popenoe, believes that there is a direct connection between fathers and child outcomes, including cognitive ability, educational achievement, psychological well-being, and social behavior.

Dad it is your job to teach your children, life principles which will shape them for their adult life and prepare them to handle their personal and professional business in a responsible manner. You might not be a teacher by profession but, you are now a teacher by possession. Listed below are some things you need to teach your children and some ideas on how to do that. This is not an exhaustive list, feel free to add to the list:

- Using Bible stories, show them the rewards and consequences for obedience and disobedience.
- Do not play with fire and electricity, respect it.
- Do not pull pots or skillets off of the stove.
- Principles of science, by doing science projects.
- Show them by example how to put safety first.
- How to be on time.
- How to practice and be prepared for events.
- How to be bold and not shy.
- How to have good eye contact when talking to others.

- How to have good manners.
- How to treat other with respect, especially adults and the elderly.
- How to make good decisions.
- How to stand, fight, and when to run.
- How to pay bills, do budgets and write checks.
- How to deal with difficult people.

Dad, it is part of your responsibility to teach them. This will enable them to be more successful in their life. You must teach them what you know.

Call to action:

- Teach them the things listed above.
- Do your own list of things you want and need to teach your children before they reach adulthood.

Chapter 7

Remember

Recall, Rejoice and Remember

Remember: To have or keep an image or idea in your mind of (something or someone from the past), to not forget (something), to keep in mind for attention or consideration. (Webster's dictionary)

"Happy is the person who knows what to remember of the past, what to enjoy in the present, and what to plan for in the future." ~ Arnold H. Glasow

Remember, the good times can only happen if you create some good times worth remembering. Being a Dad can be a blast, if you make it your priority to spend time with your children and have some fun with them. Create an atmosphere for good times by doing the following:

- Be honest and real.
- Forgive.
- Be happy, and full of joy.
- Tell your children stories about the things you used to do when you were a child, use them as lessons and for laughter.
- Don't be stressed when dealing with your children. Take five or ten minutes to de-stress or relax before dealing with them.
- Focus on the positive.
- Take your children to wonderful and amazing places.
- Enjoy them, entertain them.

Call to action:

- Have fun, have fun, and I repeat, have fun with your children.
- Enjoy them and let them enjoy you.
- Plan and take them to wonderful and amazing places.
- Write a personal list of places you would like to take your children.
- Find reasons to celebrate with children, family, and friends.

Chapter 8

Speak

Your Words Are Powerful

Speak: To say words in order to express your thoughts, feelings, opinions, etc., to someone: to talk to someone

Death and life are in the power of the tongue, and those who love it will eat its fruit. Proverbs 18:21 NKJV

"Think twice before you speak, because your words and influence will plant the seed of either success or failure in the mind of another." ~ Napoleon Hill

There are things you need to say to your children. Because you are their father, there are some things they need to hear from you. They actually believe what you say. This means what you say, has the power to influence them greatly. The bible clearly states, that you have the power of life and death in your tongue, which is the power to build or destroy. We have the ability to build our child's self-esteem. Please think about saying the following things to your child:

- I love you.
- I love you forever.
- You are handsome and strong (for the boy).
- You are pretty, beautiful and strong (for the girls).
- You are smart, you are intelligent.
- You are a leader.
- I have your back.
- I am praying and pulling for you.
- I want to be like you when I grow up.
- You can do it, don't quit.
- I will help you.

- You are awesome!
- You are going to have a great life.
- Say yes and no when appropriate.
- You are going to college, (if that is something you have planned for your child).
- Save money.
- Read your Bible.
- Do your homework.

Children need to be super encouraged by you to overcome their personal obstacles and challenges. One way to encourage them is by saying great things to them and helping them in any area they need assistance.

Call to action:

- Choose your words wisely when dealing with your children.
- Use your words to build them up.
- Be optimistic, look for the good in everything, whenever possible.
- Do a list of things you need to say to your children.

Chapter 9

Positive

Have a Positive Attitude

Positive: To think about the good qualities of someone or something: thinking that a good result will happen, hopeful or optimistic (Webster's dictionary)

For as he thinketh in his heart, so is he: Eat and drink, saith he to thee; but his heart is not with thee. Proverbs 23:7 KGV

"Once you replace negative thoughts with positive ones, you'll start having positive results." ~ Willie Nelson

"Your Attitude Determines your Altitude." ~ Zig Ziglar.

Your sons and daughters automatically think you're the greatest, until you or someone convinces them of the opposite. By remaining positive and finding creative solutions to problems, this helps your children keep a positive image of you.

I took my family to the beach, and then out to a nice restaurant to celebrate my wife's birthday. When leaving the beach, one of my daughters let me know that she left her shoes on the beach. What immediately came to my mind was the saying, "it is like finding a needle in a hay stack." I went down to the beach and looked for her shoes but, could not find them. I knew we needed her shoes to be admitted to this nice restaurant. I immediately started the creative thinking process. I decided to carry the child into the restaurant and ask for a table outside on the patio. Everything worked out in our favor. We had a beautiful birthday celebration.

Call to action:

- Do your best to remain positive and calm in every situation.
- Be creative in overcoming obstacles.
- Remember, if you can't find a needle in a hay stack, don't let it stop you from enjoying friends and family.

Chapter 10

Forget

Forget: To be unable to think of or remember (something) (Webster's dictionary)

Brethren, I do not count myself to have apprehended; but one thing *I do,* forgetting those things which are behind and reaching forward to those things which are ahead, Philippians 3:13 NKJV

"Forget the past." ~ Nelson Mandela

Dad, listed below are some ways to enjoy your sons and daughters:

- Do not concentrate on the bad, always look for the good in everything, if possible.
- Forget the past problems and move forward
- Enjoy, enjoy, and enjoy your sons and daughters. Enjoy them now because when they reach adolescence they will move on with their own lives.
- Remember, kids are one hundred percent joy, and one hundred percent work. So enjoy the fruit of your labor.
- If you train, discipline, instruct them in private or at home, they will shine for you in public.
- Be conscience about what you say about your children, your words have power. If you say my children are from hell and they are devils. They might act like devils and give you hell.
- Let the children know that you are not perfect, and that you are constantly learning. Flip a pancake and let it fall on the floor on purpose, then put it back in the pan (then throw it in the trash). Your kids will think this is hilarious.

Chapter 11

Affectionate

Affectionate: liking and caring for someone or something (Webster's dictionary)

According to NCANDS (National Child Abuse and Neglect Data Systems), whose latest statistics are for 2005, an estimated 3.3 million, referrals of child abuse or neglect were received by public social service or CPS agencies. Of these referrals, 899,000 children were confirmed to be victims of abuse or neglect (U.S. Department of Health and Human Services, 2007). That means about 12 out of every 1,000 children up to age 18 in the United States were found to be victims of maltreatment in 2005 (United States Department of Health and Human Services), 2007)

Love from the center of who you are; don't fake it. Run for dear life from evil; hold on for dear life to good. Be good friends who love deeply; practice playing second fiddle. Romans 12:10 (MSG)

Even though it is our job as Dads to train our sons and daughters, to provide structure and discipline, which all children need to become well rounded adults and have feelings of security, they also need our affection. The lack of affection can be a type of neglect and cause the child to develop slower than normal, emotionally. Dads, if you are not giving your children affection or being affectionate toward them, then they are missing out on something they need for their overall growth and wellbeing.

Give your sons and daughters hugs, kisses, high fives and warm words of affection. Affection produces chemicals in the body called endorphins. Endorphins make your children feel good, like themselves, and others. Your child needs affection from you. Give affection. Every good thing you give your child from your heart, benefits you and the child.

Call to action:

- Every once in a while tell your children you love them, even your adult children.
- Give your children affection daily, give hugs, kisses, handshakes, bear hugs, warm words of affection, affirmation, etc.
- Establish a habit of giving affection, by expressing kind and encouraging words to them.
- If you know your child needs attention or encouragement in specific areas, be available and respond to the need. Children need help or encouragement when they are being challenged in their school curriculum.

Chapter 12

Observe

Dad on Deck

Observe: To watch and sometimes also listen to (someone or something) carefully (Webster's dictionary)

Riches can disappear fast. And the king's crown doesn't stay in his family forever—so watch your business interests closely. Know the state of your flocks and your herds; Proverbs 27:23-27(TLB)

What I observed about children.

Listed are some notes of the things I have learned about children, while working as a children's minister, Royal Ranger Commander, school bus driver and summer camp assistant:

- Children love attention, so give them an abundance of it.
- Children have a very creative imagination. Be effective in figuring out ways to allow them to express themselves and their creativity. Encourage their imagination and creativity and make serious efforts not to crush it or belittle it.
- Children have a great capacity to show love and compassion.
- Children need encouraging words and a nurturing atmosphere to continue to do great things.
- They need exposure to the arts, sciences and music to help them grow intellectually.
- They need rewards for good behavior, and correction and discipline for the bad behavior.

- They need your support. Take the opportunity to show up at their events to cheer them on.
- Children have real feelings. Don't disregard their feelings as insignificant or trivial.
- Children need to talk and express their feelings. Set up an atmosphere for safe and healthy conversations.
- Children need help. Let them know that you are available to assist them when needed.

Dads, study your children, and use the information gained to tailor training to the individual child.

Chapter 13

Responsibility

Dad Wanted Alive Not Dead

Responsibility: Having the job or duty of dealing with or taking care of something or someone, able to be trusted to do what is right or to do the things that are expected or required (Webster's dictionary)

"Mothers - especially single mothers - are heroic in their efforts to raise our nation's children, but men must also take responsibility for their children and recognize the impact they have on their families' well-being." ~ Evan Bayh

But if anyone does not provide for his own, and especially for those of his household, he has denied the faith and is worse than an unbeliever. I Timothy 5:8

Dad, you must take care of yourself and your children. Responsibility is an action. That means you must be constantly improving your life and the life of your children. Sitting idle is not acceptable and never has been. You must be super productive. It is your responsibility to do the following for your children:

- Take care of them.
- Make sure they have healthy food, good housing, excellent educational opportunities and a good life.
- Make sure they live in an area free from danger.
- Work with your wife or the children's mother to provide a home with a great atmosphere for their growth.

- The word responsibility means to work to provide for your children financially.

Dads, it should not have to be said but, I will say it any way. Sign the birth certificate at birth, if it is your child, claim the child, and the responsibilities from the beginning.

Dad, your responsibility is a great one, take it seriously, by taking aggressive actions.

Read about parenting and your child's development, this will help you understand them better.

Chapter 14

Respect

Respect: A feeling of admiring someone or something that is good, valuable, important, etc. High or special regard. (Webster's dictionary)

Children, obey your parents in the Lord, for this is right. 2 "Honor your father and mother," which is the first commandment with promise: 3 "that it may be well with you and you may live long on the earth." Ephesians 6:1-3NKJV

"When you have a godly husband, a godly wife, children who respect their parents and who are loved by their parents, who provide for those children their physical and spiritual and material needs, lovingly, you have the ideal unit." ~ Jerry Falwell.

Dads, it is very important that we teach our children to first respect themselves and to respect others. They also need to be taught how to honor their mother and father. Boys need to be taught at an early age to respect their mothers, grandmothers, sisters, and other females. Girls need to be taught at an early age to respect their grandfathers, father, men and boys. Both girls and boys need to be taught not to let others disrespect them or take advantage of them. They also need to be taught to honor their mother and father, respect the elderly, and those in authority.

If our sons and daughters respect themselves and others, this will help them have better lives. Consider the following statements:

- The way we teach our children respect is by example and by instruction.
- Teach them that they have great value, that they are worth more than one hundred billion dollars, in fact they are priceless. Let them know that every life is priceless.
- Teach them that because they have value, nobody should treat them like a piece of

trash or dirt, and they should not treat others in that manner.

- They should not be treated like a punching bag that is being physically abused and should be taught not to abuse others.
- They should not be verbally abused and should not verbally abuse others.
- They should act, walk, talk, and dress like the king or queen, prince or princess, that God made them to be.
- Tell them not to allow anyone to touching them in a way the makes them feel disrespected. Nobody should be touching their body parts.
- Tell them don't be shy, speak up for yourself, and know that what you have to say has value.
- Teach the boys to allow girls, women, and elderly to go first and help them when appropriate.
- Teach boys (when age appropriate) to pump the gas for a woman, don't sit in the car while your mother, sister, wife or girlfriend pumps the gas. Get your butt up and be a respectable gentleman.

- Teach boys not to hit girls and girls not to hit boys but, always protect yourself.
- Teach your children not to do anything that will cause themselves or others harm.
- Teach the boys to respect women, don't swear or spit in a lady's presence, and stand up for women when someone is disrespecting them.
- Teach boys to respect their mothers and fathers.
- Teach daughters to respect their mothers and fathers.
- Teach children when it is appropriate to speak in the presence of an adult.
- Teach children manners and etiquette.
- Teach boys, which are young men, to treat women with respect, honor and dignity.
- Teach boys to open the door for ladies and the elderly.
- Teach your children to consider others sometimes and don't be selfish.

Chapter 15

Finish, Don't Quit

Winners Never Quit

Finish: To reach the end of (something), to stop doing (something) because it is completed. (Webster's dictionary)

Quit: Released from obligation, charge, or penalty (Webster's dictionary)

"Defeat doesn't finish a man, quit does. A man is not finished when he's defeated. He's finished when he quits." ~ Richard M. Nixon

"In soloing - as in other activities - it is far easier to start something than it is to finish it." ~ Amelia Earhart

Dads, it is important that we do not quit and that we finish the job of being an effective father. We do this by making a quality decision to finish, not quitting, and continually working on the task at hand. If you do not quit, you will see the great rewards (of finishing) that will be experienced by you, your sons, daughters, and even the world. Dad, never quit, never quit, and never give in. We must finish the job of being effective fathers.

Conclusion

Here are the most important points of each chapter. I hope and pray that this book has blessed, helped and most of all, encouraged you to be a more effective Dad. Remember, "One word, one action, and one Dad, can change a child's life forever. One child can change the world." ~ Ott Harrison Jr.

Chapter 1 Present, Present, and Accounted for Sir!

Dad, your presence and involvement is very important for the healthy development of your intelligent sons and daughters. Do not, I repeat do not, believe anything to the contrary. Your children need you.

Chapter 2 Invest, What is your ROI*?

Our children use their eyes, ears, nose, mouth, and brain to experience the world, by receiving massive amounts of information. Their brain takes this information organize, analyze, and stores it for present and future use. This information is used to develop them and their lives.

*Return on investment

Chapter 3 Forgive, the Power to Live

You must forgive, forgive, and forgive. Any relationship not incorporating this concept is doomed from the beginning. It is important Dad, that you forgive and teach your children to do the same.

Chapter 4 Effective, But Not Destructive

If your physical, mental, spiritual and financial condition is excellent, you can be more effective in assisting your sons and daughters in winning in their lives.

Chapter 5 Volunteer, Another Way to be Present

Volunteering is another way to be present. It has been said that it is not about the quantity of time, but the quality of time you spend with your children. This is partly true in the sense that it is better to spend one hour riding bikes and talking with your child, than watching TV together for ten hours and not talking.

Chapter 6 Teach, Dad on Demand

You might not be a teacher by profession, but you are now a teacher by possession. You have children that need you to teach them.

Chapter 7 Remember, Recall, Rejoice and, Remember

Dad remember the good times.

Dad, create good times that are worth remembering.

Chapter 8 Speak, Your Words Are Powerful

The fact that you are their Dad, children actually believe what you say: which means, what you say has the power to influence them greatly.

Chapter 9 Positive, Have a Positive Attitude.

Your sons and daughters automatically think you're the greatest, until you or someone else convinces them of the opposite.

"Your Attitude Determines your Altitude." ~ Zig Ziglar.

Chapter 10 Forget

Enjoy, enjoy, and enjoy your sons and daughters. Enjoy them now because when they reach adolescence they will move on to their own lives.

Chapter 11 Affectionate

Affection produces chemicals in the body called endorphins that make your children feel good about themselves and others. Your child needs affection from you.

Chapter 12 Observe, Dad on Deck

Dad, take the time to study your children. Use the information gained to tailor their training and education to each individual child.

Chapter 13 Take responsibility, Dad Wanted Alive Not Dead

Responsibility is an action.

Chapter 14 Respect

Dads, it is very important that we teach our children to first respect themselves, and to respect others.

Chapter 15 Finish, Don't Quit, Winners Never Quit

Dads, it important that we don't quit and that we finish the job of being effective fathers.

Attributes of Love

If I speak in the tongues of men or of angels, but do not have love, I am only a resounding gong or a clanging cymbal. If I have the gift of prophecy and can fathom all mysteries and all knowledge, and if I have a faith that can move mountains, but do not have love, I am nothing. If I give all I possess to the poor and give over my body to hardship that I may boast, but do not have love, I gain nothing. Love is patient, love is kind. It does not envy, it does not boast, it is not proud. It does not dishonor others, it is not self-seeking, it is not easily angered, and it keeps no record of wrongs. Love does not delight in evil but rejoices with the truth. It always protects, always trusts, always hopes, and always perseveres.

Love never fails. But where there are prophecies, they will cease; where there are tongues, they will be stilled; where there is knowledge, it will pass away. For we know in part and we prophesy in part, but when completeness comes, what is in part disappears. When I was a child, I talked like a child, I thought like a child, I reasoned like a child. When I became a man, I put the ways of childhood behind me. For now, we see only a reflection as in a mirror; then we shall see face to face. Now I know in part; then I shall know fully, even as I am fully known. And now these three remain: faith, hope and love. <u>But the greatest of these is love</u>. 1 Corinthians 13 (NIV)

I quoted this scripture to let you know that if we do all these great things for our children, we must do it from our heart and because we love them. It is also important that we make sure our children have a relationship with God through His son, Jesus. Here is a little prayer you can lead your children in, to start that relationship.

Father God, I confess Jesus as Lord, and I believe that God raised Jesus from the dead, Amen.

This simple prayer is based on the three scriptures below.

For God so loved the world, that he gave his only begotten Son, that whosoever believeth in him should not perish, but have everlasting life. John 3:16 (KJV)

[9] That if thou shalt confess with thy mouth the Lord Jesus, and shalt believe in thine heart that God hath raised him from the dead, thou shalt be saved.

[10] For with the heart man believeth unto righteousness; and with the mouth confession is made unto salvation. Roman 10:9&10 (KJV)

Websites for further research

Dad Stats | National Responsible Fatherhood Clearinghouse
*https://www.**father**hood.gov/library/**dad**-stats*

Statistics on Stay-At-Home **Dads** - National At-Home **Dad...**
athomedad.org/media-resources/statistics

Father Facts - National Fatherhood Initiative
www.fatherhood.org/father-absence-statistics

DadsWorld.com :: **Statistics** :: Parenting, Importance of ...
www.dadsworld.com/parenting-statistics/importance-of-fathers.html

Stay-At-Home **Dads** - Parents.com
www.parents.com › Parenting › Just for Dad › Issues & Trends

Journal of Applied Research on **Children** | **Children** At Risk...
digitalcommons.library.tmc.edu › Children At Risk › CHILDRENATRISK

International **Journal** of **Child**, Youth and Family Studies
journals.uvic.ca/index.php/ijcyfs

Our **Hierarchy of Needs** | Psychology Today
www.psychologytoday.com/.../our-hierarchy-needs

Stages of Social-Emotional **Development** - Erik Erikson
childdevelopmentinfo.com/child- development/erickson/

Ages & **Stages** - HealthyChildren.org
www.healthychildren.org/English/...stages/.../defaul t.asp

Developmental Milestones: Your **Child**: University of...
www.med.umich.edu/.../devmile.h

www.familyfacts.org/briefs/35/family-structure- and-childrens-education

Dad 10.0   15 Ways to Be a More Effective Dad and Still Watch the Game. By Ott Harrison Jr.,

Can be ordered from Amazon.com/kindle e-books, www.dad10.com , and the author.

Author's information:

Ott Harrison Jr.

Email: ottharrisonjr@dad10.com

Blog: Thedad10.blogspot.com

Website: www.Dad10.com

Mailing address: Po Box 1510, Perris, Ca, 92572